I0560023

Reflections
of
Bonehead Madness

Bonehead Madness Poems and Lyrics

By
Johnny Spalione

For permissions or inquiries, please contact:
John Spalione
jspalione@att.net

ISBN- 978-1-965408-82-7
Published
by
Book Writing League

Dedication

This is dedicated to the many inspirations that affected my life enough to put a pen in my hand and a mindful of laughs and memories on paper.

To the many friends and acquaintances that experienced the same events and growing pains that developed our young lives, giving me a source for limitless imagination.

To the devoted family that gave me a reason to smile, a reason to cry, a reason to be proud and humble with a distinct sense of vision.

To my wife and kids that kept me grounded and determined to provide a good life for them. The source of indefinite inspiration.

With love, I pass on a little piece of me.

Acknowledgment

The Boneheads, a group of weekend musicians that agreed to jam and allow me to transform my poems into lyrics.

For the better part of twenty plus years we jammed in dining rooms, garages and rental studios a couple nights a week, writing songs and partying as a way to wind down from the grind we each faced at work. I was the dreamer and they all let me dream.

The poetry in this book is the basis of Bonehead repertoire.

Enjoy

Table of Contents

John Songs

About True Love

I can write about the birds and the bees.
'bout how love stings a man and brings a woman to her knees.
I can tell you about Adam and Eve.
'bout how love choked a man and made a woman believe.

BUT I CAN'T TELL THE STORY ABOUT TRUE LOVE.
SO DON'T ASK ME.

I can lie about my wants and my needs.
'bout how love hurts a man and makes a woman tease.
I can shout about as I please.
'bout how love broke a man and made a woman free.

I can cry about the times I've screamed.
'bout how love fools a man and makes a woman dream.
I can cry about the times I've seen.
'bout how love used a man to make a woman breed.

BUT I CAN'T TELL THE STORY ABOUT TRUE LOVE.
SO DON'T ASK ME.

Baby I'm Still In My Prime

I'm not sad enough to write another heart breaking love song.
Not mad enough to fight all those who have done me wrong.
I just wanna say good night, Good bye and so long.
To the lady that sings me the blues.

I don't have time to waste or the energy to get high.
Won't spend a dime in haste just to idly get by.
I just wanna get a taste, have a say and fly high.
Cuz lady I've paid my dues.

I've been down that road, seen all the signs.
Tried all the angles before.
I've carried a load over the limit, slept on the living room floor.
I've been up the street, heard all the lines, tested the water in time.
I've turned up the heat, and I feel so fine.
Cuz bay I'm still in my prime.

BABY I'M STILL IN MY PRIME.
BABY I'M STILL IN MY PRIME.
ALL I ASK IS FOR SOME OF YOUR TIME.
CUZ BABY I'M STILL IN MY PRIME.

Chemical Child

I followed wet highways...Stripes signs and glare.
I kicked dead leaves in the garden...because they were there.
I molded wet sand...Laid low in the grass.
I counted falling raindrops...as the hours passed.

I travel quicker than time...Running, speeding, cheating.
Night takes my body and mind...Leaves my ego down and bleeding.
I wanted adventure...A challenge and some fun.
I explored my imagination...With the rising sun.

I'M A CHEMICAL CHILD...SUNSHINES MADNESS.
MY MEMORY BLURS WHEN YOU TURN ON THE LIGHT.
I'M A CHEMICAL CHILD...I DROWN IN SADNESS.
MY SMILES SHINES WHEN YOU TURN ON THE LIGHT.

I solved the world's problems...In a talk with myself.
In the dawn I was battered...Ready to be shelved.
I slept with my eyes wide open...Wasted, tired, life unsure.
Morning broke and I followed...I was lost, drained and hurt.

I'M A CHEMICAL CHILD...SUNSHINES MADNESS.
MY MEMORY BLURS WHEN YOU TURN ON THE LIGHT.
I'M A CHEMICAL CHILD...I DROWN IN SADNESS.
MY SMILES SHINES WHEN YOU TURN ON THE LIGHT.

Daughter Of The Moon

She steps through the shadow of the silvery moon.
Smiling at darkness with a milk white spoon.
Her style attracts the hunt, but they come too soon.
She walks away laughing, she's the daughter of the moon.

She slides into romance on a golden broom.
Runs from her heart when it starts to bloom.
She leads young romantics to their doom.
She's always changing faces, she's the daughter of the moon.

SHE'S THE DAUGHTER OF THE MOON.
YOU WON'T SEE HER AT NOON.
THE DAUGHTER OF THE MOON COMES OUT AT NIGHT.
SHE'S THE DAUGHTER OF THE MOON.
SHE WON'T SHINE TOO SOON.
THE DAUGHTER OF THE MOON TURNS ON THE LIGHT.

She shines before the light of the silvery moon.
She'll save a drowning ship from being marooned.
She'll free a butterfly from its own cocoon.
And do it with a smile, she's the daughter of the moon.

She'll strut in the tube of a big typhoon.
She'll float above the water like a red balloon.
She'll paint her smile a colorful cartoon.
And do it with style, she's the daughter of the moon.

Don't Forget Me

Nothing matters more than this ... Or compares when you imagine.
That the first kiss was just a kiss ... and not what you imagined.
You were searching in lost eyes with a burning need to explore
it should come as no surprise you were searching for much more.

Something appears to me amiss ... It's hidden in the laughter.
and your temptation to resist ... has chased you to the rafters.
You were innocent and pure with a child's urge to grow old.
You grew up brazenly and sure you would find your pot of gold.

Chorus

Don't forget I've been around ...I don't pretend to have the answers.
I will always be around ... Don't forget me when you're gone.

All things good and bad will pass All things learned must be remembered.
So the experience will last And the truth not be surrendered.
You could always melt my heart with an open and passionate soul.
You were bound to play the part and it's so hard to lose control.

Chorus

Don't forget I've been around ...I don't pretend to have the answers.
I will always be around ... Don't forget me when you're gone.

Dreams of A Traveler

Sage is the rage on these cactus pie hillsides that overlook valleys of golden green fields.

Blue is the tune of brisk winter clear skies where date palms and bare oaks reach for a feel.

Swift is the wind and the red hawk soars high like a California poppy in the springtime.

Made in the shade of a cool desert mountainside are dreams of a traveler lost in time.

Dreams of a traveler lost in time...Dreams of a traveler lost in time.

A man without a soul...a man without a mind.

Dreams of a traveler lost in time.

Sold on the road down the white line highways, embraced by the freedom of nature's call.

Down for the count and my head spinning sideways as my eyes roll back and begin to fall.

Found in the clouds seen in distant horizons, a glimpse of the shadows that make us blind.

Told of the gold that lies beyond the rainbow are the dreams of a traveler lost in time.

Dreams of a traveler lost in time...Dreams of a traveler lost in time.

A man without a soul...a man without a mind.

Dreams of a traveler lost in time.

Exit Of Innocence

Sweet dreamin' girl, Mommy's virgin pearl.
Went to the city to find a new throne.
She gave love a whirl, innocent little girl.
Now she's sorry her dreams wouldn't leave her alone.

She grew up counting stars in the wheat crops.
She blew up driving cars, pushing rain raindrops.
Now she dreams to pretend and though it seems like the end.
She may never find the reason she left her home and friends.

SHE LEFT THE CITY IN TEARS...SUCH A PITY, I HEAR.
SHE DOESN'T CARE TO DISCUSS IT.
SHE HAD TO LEAVE...SO SAD.
TO BELIEVE HOW BAD.
SHE HAS TO GO BACK TO SEE THE FACTS FOR HERSELF.
SHE'S BEEN LOST IN A DREAM, AT A COST SO IT SEEMS.
THAT WE'LL NEVER SEE HER SMILE AGAIN.
SHE TRIED IN VAIN TO SUBSIDE THE PAIN.
BUT THE EXIT OF INNOCENCE SWEPT TEARS INTO RAIN.

Sweet dreamin' girl, Mommy's virgin pearl.
Went to the city to find a new throne.
She gave love a whirl, innocent little girl.
Now she's sorry her dreams wouldn't leave her alone.
She grew up counting stars in the wheat crops.
She blew up driving cars, pushing rain raindrops.
Now she dreams to pretend and though it seems like the end.
She may never find the reason she left her home and friends.

Eyes Cold Lady

On the cool side of a hot town.

There's a warm girl turned to ice.

She's a lady beyond beauty.

She's a lady that's paid the price.

She hangs diamonds on plastic paintings.

Drives Mercedes in a twilight rage.

Puts on glamour for a favor.

Dressed in sild she steals center stage.

THAT LADY...HAS EYES COLD.

EVERYONE KNOWS AN EYES COLD LADY.

EVERYONE KNOW AN EYES COLD LADY.

THAT LADY...HAS EYES COLD.

EVERYONE KNOWS AN EYES COLD LADY.

EVERYONE KNOW AN EYES COLD LADY.

She bluffs cooly calls for manners.

Salutes respect with honesty.

She sees through lies cuz the truth is.

She's told a few just like you and me.

She's seen bad days climbed dirty hills.

Worked for nothing for a long long time

Now she's happy and pays he own bills.

She's seen freedom and it changed her mind.

THAT LADY...HAS EYES COLD.

EVERYONE KNOWS AN EYES COLD LADY.

EVERYONE KNOW AN EYES COLD LADY.

THAT LADY...HAS EYES COLD.

EVERYONE KNOWS AN EYES COLD LADY.

EVERYONE KNOW AN EYES COLD LADY.

On the cool side of a hot town.
There's a warm girl turned to ice.
She's a lady beyond beauty.
She's a lady that's paid the price.
Wall Street charmers try to buy her.
Grassroot builders have to pay.
Family men cry and lie to her.
Two bit gamblers stay away.
That lady...has eyes cold.

Face It

I have seen the darkness from the brightest side of hell.
Walked down dirty streets in names of towns I cannot tell.
Picked up on the trouble pretty ladies try to sell.
Just to throw my pennies to the bottom of the well.

I have touched the teardrops that fall down from the skies.
I've had my share of sorrows, you can see it in my eyes.
I have no time for crying so please don't sympathize.
It's time for me to grow up…It's time to realize.

NOW I HAVE TO FACE IT…FACE MY DESTINY.
FACE IT… DON'T REPLACE IT… FACE WHAT'S IN FRONT OF
ME.

I've spent a lot of money tried to by my happiness.
Now I lose incentive, so I give and take no less.
I'm lost in my adventure now I need a rest.
I've failed to meet the end, I've been second guessed.
NOW I HAVE TO FACE IT…FACE MY DESTINY.
FACE IT… DON'T REPLACE IT… FACE WHAT'S IN FRONT OF
ME.

Finally Over

When your tired mind takes a fast exit.
And disappears in lost shadows of space.
And you trudge through the swamps of confusion.
With a petrified look on your face.

When seconds become hard milestones.
On your trip into the furies of hell.
And you wonder within your illusions.
If you are able to answer the bell.

When your reasons for living fail you.
And you think you have to face a new world.
And develop a new disposition.
To cover up a past that's been hurled.

When it seems like time grew without you.
And you missed all the lessons of life.
And you have to pick up lost pieces.
To show you're as sharp as a knife.

(Chorus)
WHEN THE DREAM IS FINALLY OVER.
WILL YOU JUMP OFF THE LEDGE OR FALL?

Repeat verse

WHEN THE DREAM IS FINALLY OVER.
WILL YOU JUMP OFF THE LEDGE OR FALL?
WHEN THE DREAM IS FINALLY OVER.
WILL YOU JUMP OFF THE LEDGE OR FALL?

House Divided

Sometimes we get mired in grief and despair.
Bogged down by the fools that sadly don't care.
Sometimes there's needless pain we simply can't deny.
Buried in the doubt of our distance filled eyes.

Sometimes I feel alone and shamelessly withdrawn.
I feel the end of time is quickly coming on.
Sometimes I feel the walls of disgrace crashing in.
Because the blameless walls of scandal are paper thin.

(Chorus)

YOU CAN'T GO HOME TO A HOUSE DIVIDED.
YOU CAN'T GO HOME TO A HOUSE DIVIDED.
YOU CAN'T GO HOME TO A HOUSE DIVIDED.

Somewhere an empty dream of hope is living strong.
Because the dreamer in us all still belongs.
Somewhere the light of mercy is shining bright.
Because somewhere the underdog has won the fight.

YOU CAN'T GO HOME TO A HOUSE DIVIDED.
YOU CAN'T GO HOME TO A HOUSE DIVIDED.
YOU CAN'T GO HOME TO A HOUSE DIVIDED.
Because the bridge has been burned.
And there's spit in the wind.

How Long

How long will the color of a man's skin dictate the justice that he deserves?

Will simple lack of respect continue unjustly held in the white man's reserve?

How long will the depth of a man's pocket prescribe the nature of what he's due?

Is it greed and absence of conviction that creates a world where only rich men's dreams come true?

(chorus)

How Long   Will L.A. change her make up?
And live behind a wall made of fear.
How Long   Will L.A. feel the shake up?
Say it louder I can't hear.
How Long   Will L.A. see her dreams die?
So much lost in a cloud of smoke that night.
How Long   Will it take to reconstruct?
So many lives when so many souls have died.
Tell me L.A. How Long?

How long will the fear that's in a man's eye reflect the pain buried deep in his heart?

Will the hope and aspirations crumble lost in a city that's torn apart?

How long will skeletons from our past measure the fate of who we become?

Will the lack of progress overtake us and leave us all completely numb?

(repeat chorus)

How Long?

How long will the color of a man's skin?
Dictate the justice that he deserves.
Will simple lack of respect continue?
Unjustly held in the white man's reserve.

How long will the depth of a man's pocket?
Prescribe the nature of what he's due.
Is it greed and absence of conviction?
That creates a world where only rich men's dreams come true.

How Long   will L.A. change her make up?
And live behind a wall made of fear.
How Long   will L.A. feel the shake up?
Say it louder I can't hear.
How Long   will L.A. see her dreams die?
So much lost in a cloud of smoke that night.
How Long   Will it take to reconstruct?
So man lives when so many souls have died.
Tell me L.A. How Long?

How long will the fear that's in a man's eye?
Reflect the pain buried deep in his heart.
Will hope and aspirations crumble?
Lost in a City that's torn apart.

How long will skeletons from our past?
Measure the fate of who we become.
Will the lack of progress overtake us?
And leave us all completely numb.

How Long……?

14

I Can't See You

I can't see you.
I can't see the way you see.

I can't be you.
I can't be the way you are to me.

When you smile and walk away.
Close your eyes when you see me cry.
I wonder why…I want to die…I can't see you.

I can't see you.
I can't tell which side you're on.

I can't believe you.
I can't believe the way you are to me.

When you lie and stalk away.
Turn your back when you hear me call.
I hear you call…I want it all…I can't see you.

I can't see you.
I can't feel the way you do.

I can't be you.
I can't deal with the things you do.

When you laugh and walk away.
Turn your nose when you see me try.
I want to die…I want to fly…I can't see you.

I'm In The Mood For Love

Late at night...in the winter rains.
I call my baby home.
Like a bird in flight...or a man in sane.
I let my baby roam.
It's dark at night...and I call her name.
As I sit next to the phone.
I hold my breath in tight...Like a man in shame.
I want my baby home.

I'M IN THE MOOD FOR LOVE.
I'M IN THE MOOD TO MAKE HER HAPPY.
I'M IN THE MOOD FOR LOVE...FOR LOVE...FOR LOVE.

I get uptight...I feel the pain.
When my heart is overthrown.
Like a windy night...or speedy train.
My mid is on overload.

I get the urge to fight...I want to win the game.
Don't want to be alone.
With dreams in sight...Desire in flames.
I want my baby home.

In Between Dreams

A fallen boy perches in the haze.
Crying eyes falling from their glaze.
He fell and lost count of recent days.
A pounding heart burns in a blaze.
His only true love had had enough.
Eyes for freedom called her bluff.
A game young girl found the going rough.
So she left the game in a confused huff.
IN BETWEEN DREAMS.
IN BETWEEN DREAMS.
A calling boy working for a prize.
Called and worked and then realized.
That he who finds success is he who tries.
To be the one who laughs not the one who cries.
A searching boy drifting in the breeze.
Blind hopes rising from their knees.
A learning boy found love tough to seize.
He has learned and will rise up from his knees.
IN BETWEEN DREAMS.
IN BETWEEN DREAMS.
A rising boy that has learned to choose.
Rose above the laughter to wear new shoes.
He ran in a race he could not lose.
Cuz he's running alone and he pays his own dues.
He challenged the world and calls all the shots.
A gambling fool connects all the dots.
He's turning new dials, untying old knots.
He's got to get out before his insides rot.

Is There Life On Top Of The Mountain?

You're a tower of strength standing high above the ocean.
On top of the hill looking down at all the fools.
A compelling force pulling on my emotions.
The saving grace that is making up all the rules.

(Chorus)

IS THERE LIFE ON TOP OF THE MOUNTAIN?
DOES IT COMPARE TO SILVER OR GOLD?
IS THERE LIFE ON TOP OF THE MOUNTAIN?
WILL THE CREAM OF THE CROP GROW OLD?

You have the leading role in a rerun movie.
Starring in a classic about a two bit fool.
You're slinging your guns, shooting down all my dreams.
Riding off into the sunset like the king acting cool.

IS THERE LIFE ON TOP OF THE MOUNTAIN?
DOES IT COMPARE TO SILVER OR GOLD?
IS THERE LIFE ON TOP OF THE MOUNTAIN?
WILL THE CREAM OF THE CROP GROW OLD?

It's A Beautiful Day

Children having fun running in the streets.
Smiling in the sun at the strangers they meet.
They know they're the ones the day come to greet.
Their faces come undone so innocently sweet.

IT'S A BEAUTIFUL DAY...IN EVERY WAY.
IT'S A BEAUTIFUL DAY...IT'S A WONDERFUL DISPLAY.
WHAT CAN I SAY...IT'S A BEAUTIFUL DAY?

Old friends share joys laughing at memories.
Giggling girls and boys whistling in the breeze.
They make a cheerful noise doing as they please.
They're happy to rejoice, smiles shine with ease.

Lovers holding hands, magic in their eyes.
Love, it understands and makes the youthful wise.
Dreamers in command, happiness is their prize.
A fortune in demand, heaven in disguise.

IT'S A BEAUTIFUL DAY...IN EVERY WAY.
IT'S A BEAUTIFUL DAY...IT'S A WONDERFUL DISPLAY.
WHAT CAN I SAY...IT'S A BEAUTIFUL DAY?

Just Blow On By

This old road washes out in the rain.
Don't flood me with your tears.
Don't gloom or cloud my sunny day.
Just blow on by.

This weathered path deserves no pain.
Don't walk on me tonight dear.
Don't step on my toes or bring me to my knees.
Just blow on by dear.

YOU'D DO ME RIGHT BY LEAVING NOW.
I'D BE HAPPY IF YOU LEFT ME ALONE.
PLEASE LITTLE GIRL, DON'T MAKE ME CRY.
DON'T FOOL ME AND STEAL MY PRIDE.

This old wit gets tired in the years.
Don't bore me with your dreams.
Don't fill my head with unwanted lust.
Just blow on by.

Life Is Now

You can work or you can play with your life.
But you still have to serve the time.
You can go to bed laughing 'bout the good times you had.
To hide what you can't find.
You can rent or you can buy a piece of life.
But you still have to pay the price.
You can wait to spend all that hard earned fortune.
Or watch is fade away like old dice.

You can push away 0r grab the best from life.
But you still have to reach for it all.
You can pick your own road if you want.
Or listen for the man to make his call.
You can pretend to have a hold on life.
But you still have to stand up tall.
You can show up like the coach calling the plays.
Or watch your own dreams fall.

(Chorus)
LIFE IS NOW ... YOU CAN MOVE WITHIN IT.
NOW, DON'T LET IT PASS YOU BUY.
LIVE FOR TODAY, TO HELL WITH TOMORROW.
TAKE EACH DAY, ONE DAY AT A TIME.

You can push or you can shove your way through life.
But you still have to put up a fight.
You can go a long long way for the ride.
To choose between the wrong and the right.
You can age or you can change with the times.
But you still gotta grow.
You can hang around like a star in the sky.
And shine with something to show.
(Repeat Chorus)

Like A Man In Love

I have dust in my eyes and trust in my heart.
There's been lust on my mind right from the start.
So come a little closer, let me feel the heat.
Let me sing to your soul and sweep you off your feet.

I get a rush from your looks and a hush from your style.
Like a schoolboy's crush, I'm overcome by your smile.
So come a little closer, let me see and feel.
That little bit of magic tells me love is real.

(Chorus)

I want to kiss you…I want to hold you.
I want to make love to you…Like a Man in Love.
I want to give you my heart and soul.
I want to make love to you…Like a Man in Love.

I sense truth in my plight and youth in my desires.
And the proof is my fight to keep the spirit alive.
So come a little closer, let me rock your world.
I'll be your friend forever if you could be my girl.

Repeat Chorus

(Bridge)

But I know I can only think about it.
In the back of my mind I can dream about it.
But it's the wrong place...and wrong time to face it.
If the past were now I'd be fine and embrace it.

Repeat Chorus 2 times.

Little Boys Can't Pretend

Tommy was a victim of life.
A casualty of changing times.
Tommy grew up in a hurry.
In a hood consumed with crime.
Just like the other poor boys.
Tommy fought to pursue his dreams.
Tommy had to battle his conscience.
To beat the streets and escape the scene.
ONLY THE HOME BOYS UNDERSTAND.
TOMMY HAD TO BE A MAN.
CITY STREETS HAVE A MESSAGE TO SEND.
THAT LITTLE BOYS CAN'T PRETEND.
AND BAD BOYS LOSE IT IN THE END.
Tommy faced the dangers of life.
Taking chances with loaded dice.
Tommy thought a gun was a toy.
Thought it cool to be a man with a price.
Just like the other poor boys.
He packed his manhood in the cuff of his jeans.
Tommy fell prey to the Bad Boys mystique.
He lost control and it turned him mean.
ONLY THE HOME BOYS UNDERSTAND.
TOMMY HAD TO BE A MAN.
CITY STREETS HAVE A MESSAGE TO SEND.
THAT LITTLE BOYS CAN'T PRETEND.
AND BAD BOYS LOSE IT IN THE END.
Tommy was a victim of life.
A victim of downtrodden years.
Tommy found the end in a bullet.
Bringing truth to his Mother's fear.
Just like the other poor boys.

He was young and impressed by it all.
But in the end he was only a number.
He was a bad boy that had to fall.
ONLY THE HOME BOYS UNDERSTAND...

Locked In A Dream

A muggy winter haze swamps the worksite
Like a smoggy LA daze that makes me uptight
But it's alright…I'm in flight
And the music's got me locked in a dream.

Franky and the boys have been up all night
Playing with the toys that give 'em much delight
But it's alright…They're in flight
And the music's got 'em locked in a dream.

I'M SMILING, CUZ I FEEL GOOD
THEY'RE TRYING TO DO GOOD
WE'RE FLYING CUZ THE MUSIC'S GOT US LOCKED IN A
DREAM.

A misty morning breeze rolls on the gravesite
Like the nasty 'laskan freeze that cools the mainline
But it's alright…I'm in flight
And the music's got me locked in a dream
Harry and the guts watch the union strike
It's no big surprise you know he thought they might
But it's alright…he's in flight
And the music's got him locked in a dream

I'M SMILING, CUZ I FEEL GOOD
THEY'RE TRYING TO DO GOOD
WE'RE FLYING CUZ THE MUSIC'S GOT US LOCKED IN A
DREAM
I'M SMILING, CUZ I FEEL FREE
THEY'RE TRYING TO SATISFY ME
WE'RE FLYING CUZ THE MUSIC'S GOT US LOCKED IN A
DREAM.

Madman's Hands

Judy worked here smile to pick her way through the crowd
Serving drinks in the corner to a wild bunch talking loud
I drank the fire to be in the story, tipped heavy...a happy man
As my eyes bounced through the crowd
I learned... I was in the Madman's hands.

THE MADMAN'S HANDS
THE MADMAN'S HANDS...I WAS IN THE MADMAN'S HANDS
MY HANDS WERE SHAKING, MY HEAD WAS HOT
MY EYES WERE FALLING WITH EVERY SHOT
THE MADMAN'S HANDS.

I directed a movie, actors moved my thoughts
Judy smiles while serving, I swallowed my words and Scotch
The night moved fast and I flew with it, I held the chair with my back
When I stood I knew I was drifting into the madman's attack.

I sat on a smile, my eyes penetrating
Projecting dreams and laughing loud
I gathered my wits and vanished in the darkness
Vanished on the south side of town.

THE MADMAN'S HANDS
THE MADMAN'S HANDS...I WAS IN THE MADMAN'S HANDS
MY HANDS WERE SHAKING, MY HEAD WAS HOT
MY EYES WERE FALLING WITH EVERY SHOT
THE MADMAN'S HANDS.

Make Her Mine

She looked nasty, must have been thirty
A low cut blouse and freckles on her chest
She walked nasty, ooh she was dirty
And I wanted to meet her ... and make her mine
She spoke softly, must have been luring
A smart tongue and a sultry gaze
She spoke nasty, ooh she was flirting
And I wanted to meet her ... and make her mine.

SHE LOOKED FINE...AND I WANTED TO MAKE HER MINE.
SHE LOOKED FINE...AND I WANTER TO MAKER HER MINE.

She winked coyly, must have been laughin'
Her eyebrow raised and I caught her style
I winked boldly, I let it just happen
Cuz I wanted to meet her ... and make her mine
I walked over, must have been crazy
My mouth was dry and her lips were wet
She smiled at me, her eyelashes waving
And I wanted to meet her ... and make her mine.

SHE LOOKED FINE...AND I WANTED TO MAKE HER MINE
SHE LOOKED FINE...AND I WANTER TO MAKER HER MINE.

Man On A Mission

He stands behind issues most deplore
A Romeo player don't know the score
He walks in the spotlight, a media scene
A driven old warrior, still lean and mean.

He runs a course of destiny most decry
A perilous plight some won't deny
He drives blindly into darkness with our dreams
A candid campaigner just lettin' off steam.

MAN ON A MISSION...ON A QUEST FOR FAME
MAN ON A MISSION
MAN ON A MISSION...PLAYIN' THE GAME
MAN ON A MISSION.

He's a smooth operator in his own mind
A dreamer with a plan that's well defined
He's obsessed by the hunt and the lust for fame
He's possessed by the conquest of the game.

MAN ON A MISSION...ON A QUEST FOR FAME
MAN ON A MISSION
MAN ON A MISSION...PLAYIN' THE GAME
MAN ON A MISSION.

Message To All The Survivors

That's a blind man sittin' on the corner starin'
Clouded eyes don't see the trouble everywhere
A curious mind knows there's something there
It's a message to all the survivors
The hardened grin in his smile shows deep despair
But his whistle is sharp and it fills the air
With a song of hope for brother's everywhere
He has a message to all the survivors.

IT'S A MESSAGE OF LOVE TO THE POOR AND HOMELESS.
A MESSAGE OF HOPE FROM A RISING STAR.

There's a deaf boy standin' on the corner cryin
Sheltered ears won't hear and he don't know why
The weathered pain on his face is falling from his eye
It's a message to all the survivors
A lonely face is worn by deceit and lyin'
As he reads about the noise, he can't realize
But he still knows how to dream and fantasize
He has a message for all the survivors.

IT'S A MESSAGE OF LOVE TO THE POOR AND HOMELESS
A MESSAGE OF HOPE FROM A RISING STAR
IT'S A MESSAGE OF LOVE TO THE LOST AND FORGOTTEN
A MESSAGE TO ALL THE SURVIVORS.

That's a dumb man standin' on the corner seethin'
His bitten tongue won't tell what his lonely heart feels
His silence is a weapon he must conceal
It's message to all the survivors

His story isn't part of the plan he's dealin'
But the black and white truth is really real
He's stuck in the dirt of society's heel
with a message for all the survivors.

Moneys' Been Spent

The poets on wall street can't reach the bottom line
Their ends won't meet and their means won't rhyme
They're searching for answers but running out of time
Cuz the money's been spent and the well's gone dry
Hookers on Hyde street still show a little thigh
Their smiles run deep but their job is still a crime
Like politicians and preachers they can't spare a dime
Cuz the money's been spent and the well's gone dry.

THE MONEY'S BEEN SPENT... AND THE WELL'S GONE DRY.
THE MONEY'S BEEN SPENT... AND THE WELL'S GONE DRY.

Drifters on Broadway will tell no lies
They peddle their dreams like a teary eyed mime
And shine like a mistress that's past her prime
Cuz the money's been spent and the well's gone dry
Monkey's on Main Street won't wear a shirt and tie
They can't stand the heat and won't touch the grime
They're grasping at straws but their gin has no lime
Cuz the money's been spent and the well's gone dry.

THE MONEY'S BEEN SPENT... AND THE WELL'S GONE DRY.
THE MONEY'S BEEN SPENT... AND THE WELL'S GONE DRY.

Druggies on the Boulevard don't see the morning light
Their lessons come hard and the reward is unkind
They're searching for dreams they just won't find
Cuz the money's been spent and the well's gone dry
Coasters on the Boardwalk won't get a free ride
They'll strut on their skaes just biding their time
They'll roll along but won't reach the other side
Cuz the money's been spent and the well's gone dry.

THE MONEY'S BEEN SPENT... AND THE WELL'S GONE DRY.
THE MONEY'S BEEN SPENT... AND THE WELL'S GONE DRY.

My Escort To Hell

My escort to hell messed with my emotions
As far as I could tell it was a test of my devotions
Slowly taken for a ride into depths of mass confusion
I could not pick a side, I was swept into seclusion.

I WAS A MADMAN LOOKING FOR A CHEAP THRILL.
A MADMAN LOOKING FOR A FREE RIDE.

My escort to hell took my will and determination
Made me bid a fond farewell to my soul and inspiration
Quickly turned onto a smile that was brought on by deception
Twisted and beguiled, I knew there'd be no exceptions.

I WAS A MADMAN LOOKING FOR A CHEAP THRILL.
A MADMAN LOOKING FOR A FREE RIDE.

My escort to hell toyed with my mind's creation
My lust for life repelled into senseless contemplations
Swiftly driven by design, I promptly took on my aggressions
It was all I could find to fight off the ill suggestions.

I WAS A MADMAN LOOKING FOR A CHEAP THRILL.
A MADMAN LOOKING FOR A FREE RIDE.

Mysterious Lady

In natural tradition she responds to the show
Mature intuition, the lady knows
She likes smart conversation, answers honest Joe
For short lived relations she'll let her feelings go.

She has a straight opinion through imaginative stares
A sly inquisition shows the lady cares
She's in the new institution of people everywhere
To find a real solution puts the magic in the air.

MYSTERIOUS LADY HIDES HER BEAUTY.
MYSTERIOUS LADY HURLS A SLANTED SMILE.
MYSTERIOUS LADY SHINES IN HER DUTY.
MYSTERIOUS LADY IS A LADY IN STYLE.

She gives a direct indication, hold her chin up in the air.
Scans the presentation, she has no fear
She scopes the invitation, her smile is sincere
A dream is her creation, her doubts disappear.

MYSTERIOUS LADY HIDES HER BEAUTY.
MYSTERIOUS LADY HURLS A SLANTED SMILE
MYSTERIOUS LADY SHINES IN HER DUTY
MYSTERIOUS LADY IS A LADY IN STYLE.

Not Any Younger

I'm a bigger man now than when I thought I was so big
I conquered my fears and learned how to live
I'm a stronger man now than when I thought I was so strong
When I used to believe I could tame the world with brawn.

I'm a smarter man now than when I thought I was so smart
Time made me see a man's strength is in his heart
I'm a wiser man now that when I thought I was so wise
When I didn't know the difference between the truth and the lies.

Chorus

There's no disguisin' it or surprise in it… it's just the truth.
There's no denyin' it or reply to it… I'm past my youth.

I'm a bolder man now than when I thought I was so bold
Before I knew it was my choice to be bought or be sold
I'm a brave man now than when I thought I was so brave
I stood up to be counted and will take that to my grave.

There's no disguisin' it or surprise in it…it's just the truth
There's no denyin' it or reply to it…I'm past my youth
But I'm not any younger in my heart or mind
And not any older than dreams I left behind.
I'm not any younger than the boy I used to be
I'm not any older than the kid inside of me.

Promised Land

It was the summer of '73
My curiosity caught up to me
Opened my eyes and set my spirit free
As I prepared to leave home
I traded dreams for a walk in the park
Found my soul in my fear of the dark
I set high goals but I missed the mark
I was a long way from home
It was the summer of '73
A fire burned deep inside of me
Needed to find some company
As I set out on the road
I took the sixties challenge in stride
I was ready to experience life
But not ready to take on the strife
And burden of a heavy load.

But I knew that the mystery would pass
As I made my bed in the grass
The lessons I learned out of class
Would lead me to the promised land.

It was the summer of '73
That's when the world confronted me
I took my shot wholeheartedly
Swung hard cuz I was all alone
Went to school with the cream of the crop
Stumbled hard on my way to the top
Hoping that the dream wouldn't stop
And my heart wouldn't turn to stone.

But I knew that the mystery would pass
As I made my bed in the grass
The lessons I learned out of class
Would lead me to the promised land.

Savage In Dreamland

Life gave me a gangster's name...and a pretty boys face
My Daddy's reputation is chip I can't erase
I'm my Mamm's first creation...and proud to serve that space
I care to make my presence at the front of life's hard race.

I was a backstreet brawler...just defending my slice
I hardly saw the food side cuz I couldn't pay the price
It took time for me to realize that to fight was not so nice
But I wouldn't make the compromise...I' rather roll the dice.

Life dealt a bruised sense of humor...and a hard line of sight
I struggled with my visions... 'till I saw which side was right
I learned to make decisions...after staying up all night
Like a savage in Dreamland...who'd rather love than fight.

I'm a Savage in Dreamland...
I'm a wild man on the loose.

She Made Me Believe

She looked at me with a question in her eyes
By the tone in my voice, she was quite surprised
My subject was a dream, and she realized
That the future was in my command.

The moon shined down on my desires
Bright like the stars that had set the fire
My love for her respect could get no higher
She made me believe... I was a man.

She told me she knew 'bout the roads hard ride
But she decided it was me that'd be by her side
Steering the wheel and building her pride
Cuz the future was in her plans.

The moon shined down on my desires
Bright like the stars that had set the fire
My love for her respect could get no higher
She made me believe.. I was a man.

She Made Me Believe
She Made Me Believe
She Made Me Believe....I was a Man.

Sheba

She's thirty two and she knows how to smile
She knows how to groove cuz she remembers the style
She's cool and she thinks she knows all
But won't take the fall, make the move or the call.

It's true, her phony disguise
Those temptuous eyes won't compromise
And you think she's some kind of prize
But you don't realize the deceit and lies.

SHEBA..WILL HURT YOU LIKE NEVER BEFORE
SHEBA...SHE'S IN FOR THE GAME, NOTHING MORE
SHEBA...SHE'LL STEAL YOUR DREAMS TO MAKE HER SCORE
YOU'RE A NOTCH IN HER BELT NOW SHE'LL KICK YOU OUT
THE DOOR.

And you, you'll be counting your time
Collecting your tracks after her fierce attack
On you, you'll be counting your time
Riding that line with no sense or pride
Or rules, don't look back, she won't call
She's taken it all, you're the chain with no ball
Oh fool, don't wait to come through
It's all up to you, what you gonna do?

SHEBA..WILL HURT YOU LIKE NEVER BEFORE
SHEBA...SHE'S IN FOR THE GAME, NOTHING MORE
SHEBA...SHE'LL STEAL YOUR DREAMS TO MAKE HER SCORE
YOU'RE A NOTCH IN HER BELT NOW SHE'LL KICK YOU OUT
THE DOOR.

Shots Ring Out

Shots Ring Out...An innocent child dies
And with his spirit goes the faith that this City will rise
Shots Ring Out...A stunned family cries
Because the madness just grows, and the truth hurts us deep inside
You can't run or hide...Can't even pick a side
You just walk in fear and hope the killing subsides.

Shots Ring Out...A peace officer falls
And with his courage goes the dream and the system painly stalls
Shots Ring Out...A local hero withdraws
And with his valor goes our hope that the future's not lost
You can't run or hide...Can't even pick a side
You just walk in fear and hope the killing subsides.

Chorus

THE VIOLENCE IN THE STREETS
MUST CEASE BEFORE WE FEEL THE HEALING
THIS SENSELESS TRAVESTY MUST HALT
LET'S STOP THE BLEEDING
THE VIOLENCE IN THE STREETS
MUST CEASE BEFORE WE FEEL THE HEALING
THIS SENSELESS TRAVESTY MUST HALT.

Shots Ring Out...A crime victim pleas
And with her horror goes belief that her demise will be grieved
Shots Ring Out...A public enemy seethes
And with the terror in their eyes, we've been brought to our knees
You can't run or hide...Can't even pick a side
You just walk in fear and hope the killing subsides.

Repeat chorus

40

Shots Ring Out

Shots Ring Out...An innocent child dies
And with his spirit goes the faith that this City will rise
Shots Ring Out...A stunned family cries
Because the madness just grows and the truth hurts us deep inside
You can't run or hide...Can't even pick a side
You just walk in fear and hope the killing subsides.

Shots Ring Out...A peace officer falls
And with his courage goes the dream and system painly stalls
Shots Ring Out...A local hero withdraws
And with his valor goes our hope that the future's not lost
You can't run or hide...Can't even pick a side
You just walk in fear and hope the killing subsides.

THE VIOLENCE IN THE STREETS
MUST CEASE BEFORE WE FEEL THE HEALING
THIS SENSELESS TRAVESTY MUST HALT
LET'S STOP THE BLEEDING
THE VIOLENCE IN THE STREETS
MUST CEASE BEFORE WE FEEL THE HEALING
THIS SENSELESS TRAVESTY MUST HALT.

Shots Ring Out...a crime victim pleas
And with her horror goes belief that her demise will be grieved
Shots Ring Out...A public enemy seethes
And with the terror in their eyes we've been brought to our knees
You can't run or hide...Can't even pick a side
You just walk in fear and hope the killing subsides.

THE VIOLENCE IN THE STREETS
MUST CEASE BEFORE WE FEEL THE HEALING
THIS SENSELESS TRAVESTY MUST HALT
LET'S STOP THE BLEEDING
THE VIOLENCE IN THE STREETS
MUST CEASE BEFORE WE FEEL THE HEALING
THIS SENSELESS TRAVESTY MUST HALT.

Sleepy Eyes

You're the subject of my fantasies
The picture of my dreams
The last step to ecstasy
The coffee in my cream
Your smile is tantalizing
Your walk is teasing me
The fire in my heart is thriving
Because you do it so pleasingly.

SLEEPY EYES...YOU'LL BE MY DEMISE
IF YOU TANTALIZE...MY SLEEPY EYES
SLEEPY EYES...DON'T TELL ME LIES
MAKE ME WISE...SLEEPY EYES.

Your brow raises encouragement
You're the end of my worldly means
You're the vision of heavenly skies
The answer to my crazy dreams
You catapult me to the stars
You rocket me past the moon
If you'd listen to the wind in my heart
We'd make a slumbering landing soon.

SLEEPY EYES...YOU'LL BE MY DEMISE
IF YOU TANTALIZE...MY SLEEPY EYES
SLEEPY EYES...DON'T TELL ME LIES
MAKE ME WISE...SLEEPY EYES.

So Many Things In Life Just Aren't Fair

You want to hold back all the tears and let out all your anger
Hide behind your fears in the middle of the night
There are things you don't wanna hear
but you want to know the answer
You wish it would disappear, but you listen just in spite.

You want to pack up all your bags and hole up in your back room
just to hear them brag 'bout the story of your life
You want to close the final page and open another chapter
Put your life on center stage and stand in a brand new light.

Chorus
So Many things in life just aren't fair
So Many things in life just aren't fair
If all your dreams would come true
it would be the end of you
So Many things in life just aren't fair.

You want to lead the parade but you don't wanna hear the laughter
You just wanna make the grade and dance in the moonlight
You try hard to be brave and stand behind your actions
all the courage you can save will lead you in the fight.

Chorus

Social Girls

Angie is young and excessive
She's learned to play the game
She yearns to make name...She's a social girl
Joyce's dreams are excessive
Her desires are the same
To buy her is a shame...She's a social girl.

SHE'S A SOCIAL GIRL REACHING FOR THE LIMIT
SHE'S A SOCIAL GIRL LOOKING FOR THE GOLD
SHE'S A SOCIAL GIRL AND HER HEART IS TRULY IN IT
SHE'S A SOCIAL GIRL LOOKING FOR THE GOLD.

Joy is cool yet relentless
She tries to keep it straight
She is wise about the first dates...She's a social girl
Paula's aims are eventless
She agrees to any debate
And spare time she will donate...She's a social girl.

Kim is strong and aggressive
Cuz she needs to relate
All the dreams she creates...She's a social girl
Patte's beauty is impressive
And her smile is worth the wait
Cuz her style really rates...She's a social girl.

SHE'S A SOCIAL GIRL REACHING FOR THE LIMIT
SHE'S A SOCIAL GIRL LOOKING FOR THE GOLD
SHE'S A SOCIAL GIRL AND HER HEART IS TRULY IN IT
SHE'S A SOCIAL GIRL LOOKING FOR THE GOLD.

Spontaneous Emotions

(Kathy's Song)
Kathy wades through the masses, supporting full glasses
serving reasons for people to sway
She dodges moustaches and winking eyelashes
Serving reasons for people to say
Kathy's smile is straight, she passes it along
With her walk she could hypnotize
Her attitude is great, she passes it along
She directs her style with her eyes.

SPONTANEOUS EMOTIONS...
LIVE IN MAGIC KINGDOMS, CREATE A MYSTIC MOOD
SPONTANEOUS EMOTIONS...
TEMPT THE LONELY, ATTEMPTS TO MAKE THINGS GOOD
SPONTANEOUS EMOTIONS
SPONTANEOUS EMOTIONS.

Kathy waits on the riches, mongrels and bitches
Serving reasons for Kathy to cry
She blocks out the hisses, the superficial kisses
Serving reasons for Kathy to hide
Kathy's smile is bright, she passes it along
A crystal reflection of soul
Her attitude is right, she passes it along
An appealing joy to behold.

SPONTANEOUS EMOTIONS...
LIVE IN MAGIC KINGDOMS, CREATE A MYSTIC MOOD
SPONTANEOUS EMOTIONS...
TEMPT THE LONELY, ATTEMPTS TO MAKE THINGS GOOD
SPONTANEOUS EMOTIONS
SPONTANEOUS EMOTIONS.

Stepping Out

Walking in the shadows, she's closing in on darkness
Fancy clothes... On her toes she's stepping out
Peeking at stray lights, she's looking for direction
A stuffy nose... she's a rose... she's stepping out
Shining in her presence, a sparkling ray of light
Image of gold...acting bold...she's stepping out

SHE'S DRESSED TO KILL TO STALK THE NIGHT LIFE
BUT SHE'S JUST ANOTHER PRETTY FACE
SHE SEEKS A THRILL TO TALK ABOUT LIFE
BUT SHE'S JUST ANOTHER PRETTY FACE

A modest smile...it's a natural show
It excites me...invites me... stepping out
She gives a sensuous wing, that wink is sinister
It tempts me...it sends me...stepping out
She blows a windy kiss and something overwhelms me
It stuns me...she comes to me...stepping out

SHE'S DRESSED TO KILL TO STALK THE NIGHT LIFE
BUT SHE'S JUST ANOTHER PRETTY FACE
SHE SEEKS A THRILL TO TALK ABOUT LIFE
BUT SHE'S JUST ANOTHER PRETTY FACE

Stuck On The Image Of You

I was peeking inside the window
And I could see the writing on the wall
There was a crystal clear picture
A vision that beckoned my call
I could feel the power within me
Try to push me to the other side
But then I saw the image
Appear in the back of my mind

I'M STUCK ON THE IMAGE OF YOU
A BEAM AS I WALK THROUGH THE DOOR
LIKE A BEACON GUIDING ME HOME
I KNOW WHAT I'M LOOKING FOR

I've got a pocketful of starburst
And I bring it home just to make you smile
I know you wait my arrival
Don't you know I want to enter in style
I want to be the center of attention
So I can ride high on my pride
And bare the gift of my love
So I can be in the back of your mind

I'M STUCK ON THE IMAGE OF YOU
A BEAM AS I WALK THROUGH THE DOOR
LIKE A BEACON GUIDING ME HOME
I KNOW WHAT I'M LOOKING FOR

That's Not What I Hear

You make those empty promises like a real politician
Smiling as you speak in a gambler's tradition
You make the story sound so true to life ...But that's not what I hear
You tell the same old lies disguised as dirty laundry
Selling the evening dirt with the odds in the sports report
You state each hard fact with such conviction...But that's not what I hear

THAT'S NOT WHAT I HEAR
THAT'S NOT WHAT I WANT TO BELIEVE
THAT'S NOT WHAT I HEAR

You shed unwanted light on the dark side of history
Casting shadows on our heroes while you bask in your own glory
You recount notes you can't find in your memory... But that's not what I hear

THAT'S NOT WHAT I HEAR
THAT'S NOT WHAT I WANT TO BELIEVE
THAT'S NOT WHAT I HEAR

The Captain's Galley

Spinning in my seat, in the Captain's Galley
Holding onto life with a shaky left hand
Captain Jack would be proud of my intentions
Survival yields in this strange, strange land

I'M IN THE CAPTAIN'S GALLEY
I'M ON THE WITNESS STAND
I'M IN THE CAPTAIN'S GALLEY
SWALLOWING LIFE THE BEST I CAN

Excitement eludes me in my creative space
I'm covered with my face in a distant cloud
Blurred by innocence of my naïve dreams
I hide in inspiration to satisfy the crowd

I'm on display like brands of special house spirits
Glowing like the candles that reflect my high
Mysterious like the strange looking over my shoulder
Cold like the stared that contact my eyes

I'M IN THE CAPTAIN'S GALLEY
I'M ON THE WITNESS STAND
I'M IN THE CAPTAIN'S GALLEY
SWALLOWING LIFE THE BEST I CAN

The Mightiest Hilltopper

You walk into a crowded room
And become the center of attention
A handshake and a kiss blow through
And not a bad work mentioned
The star in your childhood dreams
Has overcome your style and walk
Almost to the top it seems
Shining above and beyond the talk

YOU'RE THE MIGHTIEST HILLTOPPER
THE KING OF THE ROADWAY
A TOW BIT SHOW TOPPER
AND YOU DID IT YOUR WAY

A proud look wears your face
Because you've had an eyeful of fame
You're the small man ahead in the race
Of the fight in a big man's game
The courage stored in your pocket
Falls out like loose change
The halo above your head
Shouldn't seem only strange
You've worked hard to be number one
Shooting above and beyond the stars
Now you're the mightiest hilltopper
So walk with a lot of heart

To Show How Much I Care

Words aren't strong enough
A song isn't soft enough
Flowers aren't pretty enough
To show how much I care
A day isn't long enough
A smile isn't bright enough
A kiss isn't quite enough
To show how much I care

I WANT YOU TO FEEL THE LOVE I HAVE TO SHARE
I WILL GIVE YO ALL MY LOVE
TO SHOW HOW MUCH I CARE
I WANT YOU TO TELL PEOPLE EVERYWHERE
THAT I GIVE YOU ALL MY LOVE TO SHOW HOW MUCH I CARE

Candy isn't sweet enough
Diamonds don't shine enough
The moon isn't full enough
To show how much I care
Tomorrow isn't soon enough
Forever won't be enough
Each second is just time enough
To show how much I care

True Friendship Never Dies

Times get tough so you reach for a friend
Life gets rough so you try to pretend
That enough is not enough
And you fight it to the end
True friendship never dies

YOU TRIED LYING TO FIND FILL IN LOVERS
YOU TRIED CRYING TO FIND FILL IN FRIENDS
YOU DIED TRYING TO FIND FILL IN HAPPINESS
CUZ YOU KNOW YOU WON'T FIND A BETTER LOVING FRIEND

Your spirits are down so you call for an old ear
You spill the old sounds and drop familiar tears
You make smiles from frowns
that have added through the years
True friendship never dies

Life comes alive, you're thankful for what you've learned
New dreams arrive and your zest for life returns
Belief stays alive as you count the love you've earned
True friendship never dies

YOU TRIED LYING TO FIND FILL IN LOVERS
YOU TRIED CRYING TO FIND FILL IN FRIENDS
YOU DIED TRYING TO FIND FILL IN HAPPINESS
CUZ YOU KNOW YOU WON'T FIND A BETTER LOVING FRIEND

Trying To Be Free

In my first try to be free…I lost sight of the kid in me
I didn't know how hard it would be 'til I tried crying
I couldn't tell where the road would go
Wouldn't sell what a stranger knows
I didn't know 'bout a row of crows…I thought the street was lying

BUT I KEPT TRYING…TRYING TO BE FREE
I KEPT BUYING LIES, TRYING TO BE FREE

In my first try to be free…I lost sight of the kid in me
I didn't know how hard it would be 'til I tried crying
When my thirst took me to the sea
I looked for fun and privacy
In my dreams and my fantasies…but I was only hiding

BUT I KEPT TRYING…TRYING TO BE FREE
I KEPT BUYING LIES, TRYING TO BE FREE

In my first try to be free…I lost sight of the kid in me
I didn't know how hard it would be 'til I tried crying
Then my search for reality
Took me through the galaxy
Now not just you, but I can see that I was merely hiding

BUT I KEPT TRYING…TRYING TO BE FREE
I KEPT BUYING LIES, TRYING TO BE FREE

Turn On The Light

In the middle of the night in a hot coast city
Where the stars don't shine cuz the lights are too bright
I'm sitting on my pride trying to find to find myself
Trying to see tomorrow before the sun sheds light

Hours pass by and the city hurries after
The moon hides away behind the dawning day
I'm wondering about the magic that has disappeared
Trying to find love before it slips away

I'M LOOKING FOR YOU...TO TURN ON THE LIGHT
I'M LOOKING FOR YOU ...TO MAKE ME FEEL RIGHT
I'M LOOKING FOR YOU... TO TURN ON THE LIGHT

In the middle of a dream in a hot cold sweat
Where life comes alive in memory of a song
I'm listening to my heart trying to hear the beat
Trying to hear the tune before it moves along

Pictures flash by and my mind soon after
The past comes back in a haunting way
I'm wondering about the magic that has disappeared
Trying to find love before it slips away

I'M LOOKING FOR YOU...TO TURN ON THE LIGHT
I'M LOOKING FOR YOU ...TO MAKE ME FEEL RIGHT
I'M LOOKING FOR YOU... TO TURN ON THE LIGHT

Values, Morals, Ethics

Hard times come and the money goes
Crime has won and the wear and tear shows
The ozone succumbs and the world famine grows...there's no pity
The housing booms grind and the rainforests fall
Homeless whine and democracy calls
A change is due to find that the system stalls...in the city
The jury hangs and the victims all lose
Fury dangles like the evening news
Truth gets lost in the lies we choose...to believe in
Fast times fly and the story line blooms
The old school dies and the future looms
'till society tries to light the gloom...in the city

VALUES, MORALS, ETHICS
ALL GO OUT THE WINDOW AT THE FIRST SIGN OF MONEY
WE BASE ALL OUR DECISIONS
ON DISTORTED GOALS AND VISIONS...CUZ THE MONEY,
YEAH

Love truth and friendship
All lose their meaning at the first sign of money
Our policies will tell ya,
We're out to cheat and sell ya..cuz the money
Money! The root of all evil... the dealer of death
Money! The root of my sorrows... it's taking my breath

Chivalry and dignity
All go down the toilet at the first sign of money
Options and securities wash out in the rain...cuz the money!
Romance and honesty
Take a back seat at the first sign of money
Freedom and fantasy fall into our dreams... cuz the money!

Voice Of Reason

I was listening to you... the voice of reason
Thinking about the time you were right before
I can hear all the words, see the same old picture
That smile on your face could say no more

I was listening to you... the voice of reason
Gambling with my dreams, I was leaning with my heart
I would fight to no end to have you believing
I'm trying to make a make a choice and that's a start

Chorus

and this is my way of telling you
I respect your view, and I hear you
This is my way of showing you
I believe in you...and I love you

I was listening to you... the voice of reason
Trying to figure out how to even the score
I can only express my deepest feelings
And trust in your word forever more

Chorus

I was listening to you... the voice of reason
Thinking about the time you were right before
I can hear all the words, see the same old picture
That smile on your face could say no more

Wake Up And Die Right

Mama turned her eyes, turned her eyes, turned her eyes
And our spines crawled on the floor
She told us don't tell lies, don't tell lies, don't tell lies
And we'd be adding up the score
But before we realize, realize, realize
That her word meant even more
The truth we'd soon despise, soon despise, soon despise
Saw us walking out the door

WAKE UP..WAKE UP AND DIE RIGHT..DIE RIGHT
WAKE AND DIE RIGHT
WAKE UP...WAKE UP AND DIE RIGHT...DIE RIGHT
WAKE UP AND DIE RIGHT

Mama never teased, never teased, never tease
She always stood her ground
As long as she was pleased, she was pleased, she was pleased
Her love could sure be found
When her sanity was seized, was seized, was seized
Our freedom became bound
Her grip became a squeeze, a squeeze, a squeeze
And we'd hear that same old sound

WAKE UP..WAKE UP AND DIE RIGHT..DIE RIGHT
WAKE AND DIE RIGHT
WAKE UP...WAKE UP AND DIE RIGHT...DIE RIGHT
WAKE UP AND DIE RIGHT

What Makes You Think You Deserve Me?

If you leave your smile outside the front door
And bring me a frown as you walk across the floor
Don't you think I know you're not thinking of me?
There's distance in your eyes, it's easy to see
If you've lost a dream and you don't know where
You forgot how to laugh cuz you don't know how to care
What makes you think you can let thigs be?
What makes you think you deserve me?

WHAT MAKES YOU THINK YOU DESERVE ME?
WHAT MAKES YOU THINK YOU'RE SO FINE?
WHAT MAKES YOU THINK YOR DESERVE ME?
WHAT MAKES YOU THINK YOU'RE SO RIGHT?

If I bring you my love and you send it away
Cuz you're tired and bored, got no more to say
Is there more to life? Do you want to be free?
Is the feeling gone? Have you stopped loving me?
If the good turns bad and the nights grow old
And you become restless and the truth is untold
What makes you think you can fool me?
What makes you think you deserve me?

Where Do We Go?

I loose my lip
I tuck my brow
I can dream of Reggae music
I shake my hip
I'm on the prowl
I can play Reggae music

WHERE DO WE GO?
WE'RE PLAYING REGGAE MUSIC
HOW DID WE KNOW?
WE'RE PLAYING REGGAE MUSIC

I can't get lost
I've got my honey
We can play with Reggae music
At any cost
We're in the money
We can play with Reggae music

I close my eyes
I mix my thoughts
And dream of Reggae music
Can't sympathize
We've left the rock
We can play with Reggae music

WHERE DO WE GO?
WE'RE PLAYING REGGAE MUSIC
HOW DID WE KNOW?
WE'RE PLAYING REGGAE MUSIC.

Witch Song

She was staring deep inside a glass of wine.
And I could tell that my troubles weren't far behind.
She had distance in her eyes, I had moving on my mind.
We felt the presence of another bleeding heart.

She was holding on tight to a vacant glace
And I could tell she was looking for a dancer
She had romance in her eyes, I had moving on my mind
We felt the presence of each other's bleeding heart.

She was a witch from the south side that flew in from the north
And caught me with my guard down
I turn into a hound every time I get around other women
She was a witch from the south that flew in from the north
And caught me with my guard down
I turn into a hound every time I get around other women.

She was floating high above the smokey scene
And I could tell that this woman wasn't green
She had visions in her eyes, I had moving on my mind
We felt the presence of another bleeding heart

She was glaring deep inside an empty glass
And I could tell she was moving very fast
She had leaving in her eyes, I had moving on my mind
We felt the presence of another bleeding heart

She was a witch…..

www.ingramcontent.com/pod-product-compliance
Lightning Source LLC
Chambersburg PA
CBHW051333120626
46547CB00016B/2520